Emotional Wellness
JOURNAL

This journal belongs to

_____

The majority of this journal is designed for you to be able to pick and choose which sections will be useful to you. This will vary from day to day.

This first section, however, is slightly different. The Daily Pages section means exactly that. The recommendation is that you fill in one page every day to get a better understanding of how you feel and what's going on in your life. From this you'll learn about the the things you need to let go of and get used to using writing to help you do this.

There is space for 50 days in this section. But don't worry if you miss a day.

DATE: _____

What do you want to remember?

I feel: _____

Because: _____

Can you control it?

Think about the things causing you to stress or worry right now. Decide whether you can control the outcomes or not.

Things I can control	Things I can't control
○	○
○	○
○	○
○	○

If you can't control it, does it deserve your energy?

Words that describe life today

Ideas & Thoughts

DATE: _____

What do you want to remember?

_____
_____
_____
_____

I feel: _____

Because: _____

Can you control it? Think about the things causing you to stress or worry right now. Decide whether you can control the outcomes or not.

Things I can control | ### Things I can't control

○ _____   ○ _____
○ _____   ○ _____
○ _____   ○ _____
○ _____   ○ _____

If you can't control it, does it deserve your energy?

Words that describe life today

Ideas & Thoughts

DATE: _____

What do you want to remember?
_____
_____
_____
_____

I feel: _____

Because: _____

Can you control it? Think about the things causing you to stress or worry right now. Decide whether you can control the outcomes or not.

Things I can control	Things I can't control
○	○
○	○
○	○
○	○

If you can't control it, does it deserve your energy?

Words that describe life today	Ideas & Thoughts

DATE: _____

What do you want to remember?

_____
_____
_____
_____

I feel: _____

Because: _____

Can you control it?

Think about the things causing you to stress or worry right now. Decide whether you can control the outcomes or not.

Things I can control	Things I can't control
○	○
○	○
○	○
○	○

If you can't control it, does it deserve your energy?

Words that describe life today

Ideas & Thoughts

DATE: _____

What do you want to remember?

I feel: _____

Because: _____

Can you control it?

Think about the things causing you to stress or worry right now. Decide whether you can control the outcomes or not.

Things I can control	Things I can't control
○	○
○	○
○	○
○	○

If you can't control it, does it deserve your energy?

Words that describe life today	Ideas & Thoughts

DATE: _____

What do you want to remember?
_____
_____
_____
_____

I feel: _____

Because: _____

Can you control it? Think about the things causing you to stress or worry right now. Decide whether you can control the outcomes or not.

Things I can control
○
○
○
○

Things I can't control
○
○
○
○

If you can't control it, does it deserve your energy?

Words that describe life today

_____
_____
_____

Ideas & Thoughts

DATE: _____

What do you want to remember?

_____
_____
_____
_____

I feel: _____

Because: _____

Can you control it? Think about the things causing you to stress or worry right now. Decide whether you can control the outcomes or not.

Things I can control	Things I can't control
○	○
○	○
○	○
○	○

If you can't control it, does it deserve your energy?

Words that describe life today	Ideas & Thoughts

DATE: _____

What do you want to remember?

_____
_____
_____
_____

I feel: _____

Because: _____

Can you control it?

Think about the things causing you to stress or worry right now. Decide whether you can control the outcomes or not.

Things I can control	**Things I can't control**
○	○
○	○
○	○
○	○

If you can't control it, does it deserve your energy?

Words that describe life today	Ideas & Thoughts

DATE: _____

What do you want to remember?

_____
_____
_____
_____

I feel: _____

Because: _____

Can you control it? Think about the things causing you to stress or worry right now. Decide whether you can control the outcomes or not.

Things I can control	Things I can't control
○	○
○	○
○	○
○	○

If you can't control it, does it deserve your energy?

Words that describe life today	Ideas & Thoughts

DATE: _____

What do you want to remember?

_____
_____
_____
_____

I feel: _____

Because: _____

Can you control it? Think about the things causing you to stress or worry right now. Decide whether you can control the outcomes or not.

Things I can control   ### Things I can't control

○   ○
○   ○
○   ○
○   ○

If you can't control it, does it deserve your energy?

Words that describe life today	Ideas & Thoughts

DATE: _____

What do you want to remember?

_____
_____
_____
_____

I feel: _____

Because: _____

Can you control it?

Think about the things causing you to stress or worry right now. Decide whether you can control the outcomes or not.

Things I can control	**Things I can't control**
○	○
○	○
○	○
○	○

If you can't control it, does it deserve your energy?

Words that describe life today	Ideas & Thoughts

DATE: _____

What do you want to remember?

_____
_____
_____
_____

I feel: _____

Because: _____

Can you control it?

Think about the things causing you to stress or worry right now. Decide whether you can control the outcomes or not.

Things I can control | **Things I can't control**

○ | ○
○ | ○
○ | ○
○ | ○

If you can't control it, does it deserve your energy?

Words that describe life today

Ideas & Thoughts

DATE: _____

What do you want to remember?

_____
_____
_____
_____

I feel: _____

Because: _____

Can you control it? Think about the things causing you to stress or worry right now. Decide whether you can control the outcomes or not.

Things I can control

- ○
- ○
- ○
- ○

Things I can't control

- ○
- ○
- ○
- ○

If you can't control it, does it deserve your energy?

Words that describe life today

Ideas & Thoughts

DATE: _____

What do you want to remember?
_____
_____
_____
_____

I feel: _____

Because: _____

Can you control it? Think about the things causing you to stress or worry right now. Decide whether you can control the outcomes or not.

Things I can control	Things I can't control
○	○
○	○
○	○
○	○

If you can't control it, does it deserve your energy?

Words that describe life today

Ideas & Thoughts

DATE: _____

What do you want to remember?

I feel: _____

Because: _____

Can you control it? Think about the things causing you to stress or worry right now. Decide whether you can control the outcomes or not.

Things I can control

- ○
- ○
- ○
- ○

Things I can't control

- ○
- ○
- ○
- ○

If you can't control it, does it deserve your energy?

Words that describe life today

Ideas & Thoughts

DATE: _____

What do you want to remember?

_____
_____
_____
_____
_____

I feel: _____

Because: _____

Can you control it?

Think about the things causing you to stress or worry right now. Decide whether you can control the outcomes or not.

Things I can control	**Things I can't control**
○	○
○	○
○	○
○	○

If you can't control it, does it deserve your energy?

Words that describe life today	Ideas & Thoughts

DATE: _____

What do you want to remember?

I feel: _____

Because: _____

Can you control it?

Think about the things causing you to stress or worry right now. Decide whether you can control the outcomes or not.

Things I can control	Things I can't control
○	○
○	○
○	○
○	○

If you can't control it, does it deserve your energy?

Words that describe life today	Ideas & Thoughts

DATE: _____

What do you want to remember?

_____
_____
_____
_____
_____

I feel: _____

Because: _____

Can you control it?

Think about the things causing you to stress or worry right now. Decide whether you can control the outcomes or not.

Things I can control	Things I can't control
○	○
○	○
○	○
○	○

If you can't control it, does it deserve your energy?

Words that describe life today

_____
_____
_____

Ideas & Thoughts

DATE: _____

What do you want to remember?

_____
_____
_____
_____

I feel: _____

Because: _____

Can you control it?

Think about the things causing you to stress or worry right now. Decide whether you can control the outcomes or not.

Things I can control	Things I can't control
○	○
○	○
○	○
○	○

If you can't control it, does it deserve your energy?

Words that describe life today	Ideas & Thoughts

DATE: _____

What do you want to remember?
_____
_____
_____
_____

I feel: _____

Because: _____

Can you control it?

Think about the things causing you to stress or worry right now. Decide whether you can control the outcomes or not.

Things I can control	**Things I can't control**
○	○
○	○
○	○
○	○

If you can't control it, does it deserve your energy?

Words that describe life today

_____
_____
_____

Ideas & Thoughts

DATE: _____

What do you want to remember?

I feel: _____

Because: _____

Can you control it?

Think about the things causing you to stress or worry right now. Decide whether you can control the outcomes or not.

Things I can control	Things I can't control
○	○
○	○
○	○
○	○

If you can't control it, does it deserve your energy?

Words that describe life today	Ideas & Thoughts

DATE: _____

What do you want to remember?

_____
_____
_____
_____

I feel: _____

Because: _____

Can you control it?

Think about the things causing you to stress or worry right now. Decide whether you can control the outcomes or not.

Things I can control	Things I can't control
○	○
○	○
○	○
○	○

If you can't control it, does it deserve your energy?

Words that describe life today

Ideas & Thoughts

DATE: _____

What do you want to remember?
_____
_____
_____
_____

I feel: _____

Because: _____

Can you control it?

Think about the things causing you to stress or worry right now. Decide whether you can control the outcomes or not.

Things I can control	Things I can't control
○	○
○	○
○	○
○	○

If you can't control it, does it deserve your energy?

Words that describe life today

Ideas & Thoughts

DATE: _____

What do you want to remember?

_____
_____
_____
_____
_____

I feel: _____

Because: _____

Can you control it? Think about the things causing you to stress or worry right now. Decide whether you can control the outcomes or not.

Things I can control   Things I can't control

○ _____   ○ _____

○ _____   ○ _____

○ _____   ○ _____

○ _____   ○ _____

If you can't control it, does it deserve your energy?

Words that describe life today

Ideas & Thoughts

DATE: _____

What do you want to remember?

I feel: _____

Because: _____

Can you control it?

Think about the things causing you to stress or worry right now. Decide whether you can control the outcomes or not.

Things I can control	**Things I can't control**
○	○
○	○
○	○
○	○

If you can't control it, does it deserve your energy?

Words that describe life today

Ideas & Thoughts

DATE: _____

What do you want to remember?

_____
_____
_____
_____

I feel: _____

Because: _____

Can you control it?

Think about the things causing you to stress or worry right now. Decide whether you can control the outcomes or not.

Things I can control   **Things I can't control**

○   ○

○   ○

○   ○

○   ○

If you can't control it, does it deserve your energy?

Words that describe life today

Ideas & Thoughts

DATE: _____

What do you want to remember?
_____
_____
_____
_____

I feel: _____

Because: _____

Can you control it? Think about the things causing you to stress or worry right now. Decide whether you can control the outcomes or not.

Things I can control | Things I can't control

○   ○

○   ○

○   ○

○   ○

If you can't control it, does it deserve your energy?

Words that describe life today

Ideas & Thoughts

DATE: _____

What do you want to remember?

_____
_____
_____
_____

I feel: _____

Because: _____

Can you control it?

Think about the things causing you to stress or worry right now. Decide whether you can control the outcomes or not.

Things I can control	**Things I can't control**
○	○
○	○
○	○
○	○

If you can't control it, does it deserve your energy?

Words that describe life today

Ideas & Thoughts

DATE: _____

What do you want to remember?

_____
_____
_____
_____

I feel: _____

Because: _____

Can you control it? Think about the things causing you to stress or worry right now. Decide whether you can control the outcomes or not.

Things I can control
- ○
- ○
- ○
- ○

Things I can't control
- ○
- ○
- ○
- ○

If you can't control it, does it deserve your energy?

Words that describe life today

Ideas & Thoughts

DATE: _____

What do you want to remember?
_____
_____
_____
_____

I feel: _____

Because: _____

Can you control it? Think about the things causing you to stress or worry right now. Decide whether you can control the outcomes or not.

Things I can control
○
○
○
○

Things I can't control
○
○
○
○

If you can't control it, does it deserve your energy?

Words that describe life today

Ideas & Thoughts

DATE: _____

What do you want to remember?

I feel: _____

Because: _____

Can you control it? Think about the things causing you to stress or worry right now. Decide whether you can control the outcomes or not.

Things I can control   Things I can't control

○   ○
○   ○
○   ○
○   ○

If you can't control it, does it deserve your energy?

Words that describe life today

Ideas & Thoughts

DATE: _____

What do you want to remember?
_____
_____
_____
_____
_____

I feel: _____

Because: _____

Can you control it?

Think about the things causing you to stress or worry right now. Decide whether you can control the outcomes or not.

Things I can control	Things I can't control
○	○
○	○
○	○
○	○

If you can't control it, does it deserve your energy?

Words that describe life today

Ideas & Thoughts

DATE: _____

What do you want to remember?

I feel: _____

Because: _____

Can you control it?

Think about the things causing you to stress or worry right now. Decide whether you can control the outcomes or not.

Things I can control	Things I can't control
○	○
○	○
○	○
○	○

If you can't control it, does it deserve your energy?

Words that describe life today	Ideas & Thoughts

DATE: _____

What do you want to remember?

_____
_____
_____
_____

I feel: _____

Because: _____

Can you control it? Think about the things causing you to stress or worry right now. Decide whether you can control the outcomes or not.

Things I can control	Things I can't control
○	○
○	○
○	○
○	○

If you can't control it, does it deserve your energy?

Words that describe life today	Ideas & Thoughts

DATE: _____

What do you want to remember?

I feel: _____

Because: _____

Can you control it?

Think about the things causing you to stress or worry right now. Decide whether you can control the outcomes or not.

Things I can control	Things I can't control
○	○
○	○
○	○
○	○

If you can't control it, does it deserve your energy?

Words that describe life today	Ideas & Thoughts

DATE: _____

What do you want to remember?
_____
_____
_____
_____
_____

I feel: _____

Because: _____

Can you control it? Think about the things causing you to stress or worry right now. Decide whether you can control the outcomes or not.

Things I can control   ### Things I can't control

○ _____   ○ _____
○ _____   ○ _____
○ _____   ○ _____
○ _____   ○ _____

If you can't control it, does it deserve your energy?

Words that describe life today

Ideas & Thoughts

DATE: _____

What do you want to remember?

_____
_____
_____
_____

I feel: _____

Because: _____

Can you control it?

Think about the things causing you to stress or worry right now. Decide whether you can control the outcomes or not.

Things I can control	Things I can't control
○	○
○	○
○	○
○	○

If you can't control it, does it deserve your energy?

Words that describe life today	Ideas & Thoughts

DATE: _____

What do you want to remember?
_____
_____
_____
_____

I feel: _____

Because: _____

Can you control it? Think about the things causing you to stress or worry right now. Decide whether you can control the outcomes or not.

Things I can control	Things I can't control
○	○
○	○
○	○
○	○

If you can't control it, does it deserve your energy?

Words that describe life today

Ideas & Thoughts

DATE: _____

What do you want to remember?
_____
_____
_____
_____

I feel: _____

Because: _____

Can you control it?

Think about the things causing you to stress or worry right now. Decide whether you can control the outcomes or not.

Things I can control	Things I can't control
○	○
○	○
○	○
○	○

If you can't control it, does it deserve your energy?

Words that describe life today	Ideas & Thoughts

DATE: _____

What do you want to remember?
_____
_____
_____
_____

I feel: _____

Because: _____

Can you control it?

Think about the things causing you to stress or worry right now. Decide whether you can control the outcomes or not.

Things I can control	Things I can't control
○	○
○	○
○	○
○	○

If you can't control it, does it deserve your energy?

Words that describe life today

Ideas & Thoughts

DATE: _____

What do you want to remember?

_____
_____
_____
_____

I feel: _____

Because: _____

Can you control it?

Think about the things causing you to stress or worry right now. Decide whether you can control the outcomes or not.

Things I can control	Things I can't control
○	○
○	○
○	○
○	○

If you can't control it, does it deserve your energy?

Words that describe life today

Ideas & Thoughts

DATE: _____

What do you want to remember?

_____
_____
_____
_____

I feel: _____

Because: _____

Can you control it?

Think about the things causing you to stress or worry right now. Decide whether you can control the outcomes or not.

Things I can control	Things I can't control
○	○
○	○
○	○
○	○

If you can't control it, does it deserve your energy?

Words that describe life today

Ideas & Thoughts

DATE: _____

What do you want to remember?

_____
_____
_____
_____

I feel: _____

Because: _____

Can you control it?

Think about the things causing you to stress or worry right now. Decide whether you can control the outcomes or not.

Things I can control

- ○
- ○
- ○
- ○

Things I can't control

- ○
- ○
- ○
- ○

If you can't control it, does it deserve your energy?

Words that describe life today

Ideas & Thoughts

DATE: _____

What do you want to remember?

I feel: _____

Because: _____

Can you control it? Think about the things causing you to stress or worry right now. Decide whether you can control the outcomes or not.

Things I can control	Things I can't control
○	○
○	○
○	○
○	○

If you can't control it, does it deserve your energy?

Words that describe life today	Ideas & Thoughts

DATE: _____

What do you want to remember?

_____
_____
_____
_____

I feel: _____

Because: _____

Can you control it?

Think about the things causing you to stress or worry right now. Decide whether you can control the outcomes or not.

Things I can control	Things I can't control
○	○
○	○
○	○
○	○

If you can't control it, does it deserve your energy?

Words that describe life today	Ideas & Thoughts

DATE: _____

What do you want to remember?

_____
_____
_____
_____

I feel: _____

Because: _____

Can you control it?

Think about the things causing you to stress or worry right now. Decide whether you can control the outcomes or not.

Things I can control	Things I can't control
○	○
○	○
○	○
○	○

If you can't control it, does it deserve your energy?

Words that describe life today

_____
_____
_____

Ideas & Thoughts

DATE: _____

What do you want to remember?

_____
_____
_____
_____

I feel: _____

Because: _____

Can you control it? Think about the things causing you to stress or worry right now. Decide whether you can control the outcomes or not.

Things I can control
- ○
- ○
- ○
- ○

Things I can't control
- ○
- ○
- ○
- ○

If you can't control it, does it deserve your energy?

Words that describe life today

Ideas & Thoughts

DATE: _____

What do you want to remember?
_____
_____
_____
_____

I feel: _____

Because: _____

Can you control it? Think about the things causing you to stress or worry right now. Decide whether you can control the outcomes or not.

Things I can control
○
○
○
○

Things I can't control
○
○
○
○

If you can't control it, does it deserve your energy?

Words that describe life today

Ideas & Thoughts

DATE: _____

What do you want to remember?
_____
_____
_____
_____

I feel: _____

Because: _____

Can you control it? Think about the things causing you to stress or worry right now. Decide whether you can control the outcomes or not.

Things I can control
-
-
-
-

Things I can't control
-
-
-
-

If you can't control it, does it deserve your energy?

Words that describe life today

Ideas & Thoughts

DATE: _____

What do you want to remember?

_____
_____
_____
_____
_____

I feel: _____

Because: _____

Can you control it?

Think about the things causing you to stress or worry right now. Decide whether you can control the outcomes or not.

Things I can control	**Things I can't control**
○	○
○	○
○	○
○	○

If you can't control it, does it deserve your energy?

Words that describe life today

Ideas & Thoughts

DATE: _____

What do you want to remember?
_____
_____
_____
_____

I feel: _____

Because: _____

Can you control it?

Think about the things causing you to stress or worry right now. Decide whether you can control the outcomes or not.

Things I can control	Things I can't control
○	○
○	○
○	○
○	○

If you can't control it, does it deserve your energy?

Words that describe life today

Ideas & Thoughts

DATE: _____

What do you want to remember?

_____
_____
_____
_____

I feel: _____

Because: _____

Can you control it?

Think about the things causing you to stress or worry right now. Decide whether you can control the outcomes or not.

Things I can control	Things I can't control
○	○
○	○
○	○
○	○

If you can't control it, does it deserve your energy?

Words that describe life today

Ideas & Thoughts

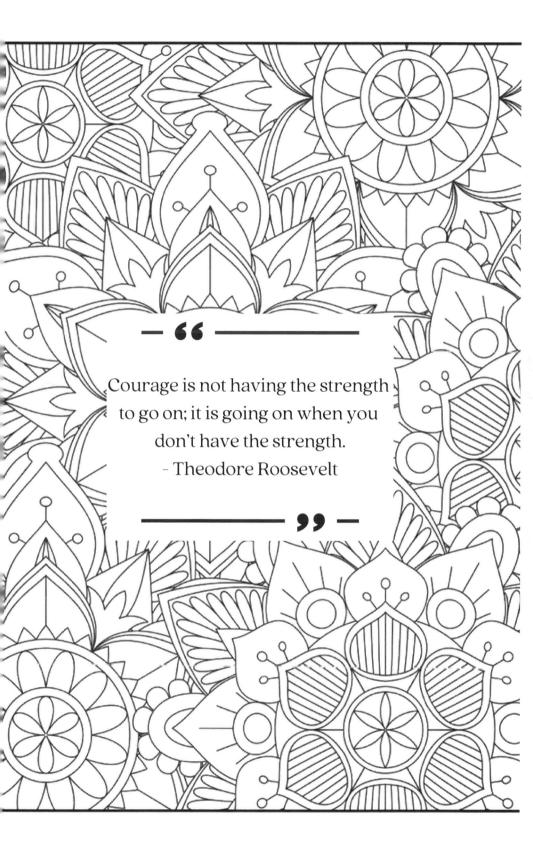

The Prompt Me section is designed to really get you thinking about life, yourself and how you feel.

In the pages that follow, you'll find tons of hand-picked prompts to get you writing. There is plenty of space so just write anything and everything that enters your head.

There are no limitations or expectations in this section. Free yourself and let go.

WHAT IS ONE THING FROM YOUR PAST THAT YOU FEEL LIKE YOU NEED TO LET GO OF?

_____
_____
_____
_____
_____
_____
_____
_____
_____
_____
_____
_____
_____
_____
_____
_____
_____
_____
_____
_____
_____

LET IT GO

WHAT IS ONE THING THAT IS CURRENTLY WORRYING YOU THE MOST? CAN YOU CONTROL IT?

FREE YOURSELF

WHAT DO YOU NEED TO FORGIVE YOURSELF FOR?

Free write about this & see what comes out

_____
_____
_____
_____
_____
_____
_____
_____
_____
_____
_____
_____
_____
_____
_____
_____
_____
_____
_____
_____
_____
_____

LET IT GO

HOW CAN YOU BE AT LEAST 5% KINDER TO YOURSELF EVERY SINGLE DAY?

FREE YOURSELF

KEEP WRITING: THINGS MIGHT NOT ALWAYS GO SMOOTHLY BUT AT LEAST...

LET IT GO

FREE WRITE ABOUT THE BIGGEST CHALLENGE YOU ARE FACING IN LIFE RIGHT NOW

_____
_____
_____
_____
_____
_____
_____
_____
_____
_____
_____
_____
_____
_____
_____
_____
_____
_____
_____
_____
_____
_____
_____

FREE YOURSELF

WHAT IS ONE LIMITING BELIEF YOU HOLD ABOUT YOURSELF? IS IT TRUE? CAN YOU LET IT GO?

_____
_____
_____
_____
_____
_____
_____
_____
_____
_____
_____
_____
_____
_____
_____
_____
_____
_____
_____
_____

LET IT GO

WHAT IF YOU NEVER HAD ANYTHING TO WORRY ABOUT? WHAT WOULD LIFE BE LIKE?

_____
_____
_____
_____
_____
_____
_____
_____
_____
_____
_____
_____
_____
_____
_____
_____
_____
_____

FREE YOURSELF

WRITE ABOUT SOMETHING YOU'VE MOVED ON FROM THAT USED TO MEAN THE WORLD TO YOU AT SOME POINT

_____
_____
_____
_____
_____
_____
_____
_____
_____
_____
_____
_____
_____
_____
_____
_____
_____
_____
_____
_____

LET IT GO

WHAT IS SOMETHING BIG YOU'VE ACHIEVED THAT YOU ONCE BELIEVED WAS IMPOSSIBLE?

_____
_____
_____
_____
_____
_____
_____
_____
_____
_____
_____
_____
_____
_____
_____
_____
_____
_____
_____

FREE YOURSELF

WHAT CAN YOU LEARN FROM YOUR BIGGEST MISTAKES (INSTEAD OF HOLDING ON/WORRYING ABOUT THEM)?

_____
_____
_____
_____
_____
_____
_____
_____
_____
_____
_____
_____
_____
_____
_____
_____
_____
_____
_____
_____
_____

LET IT GO

WRITE A BIG LIST OF ABSOLUTELY EVERYTHING YOU WANT TO SAY NO TO.

FREE YOURSELF

IF YOU NEVER HAD TO WORRY ABOUT MONEY OR OPINIONS, WHAT WOULD YOU DO WITH YOUR LIFE? WHY?

LET IT GO

WRITE A BIG LIST OF ABSOLUTELY EVERYTHING YOU WANT TO SAY YES TO.

FREE YOURSELF

WHAT IS SOMETHING THAT DOESN'T MAKE ANY SENSE WHATSOEVER IN YOUR LIFE?

_____

_____

_____

_____

_____

_____

_____

_____

_____

_____

_____

_____

_____

_____

_____

_____

_____

_____

_____

_____

_____

LET IT GO

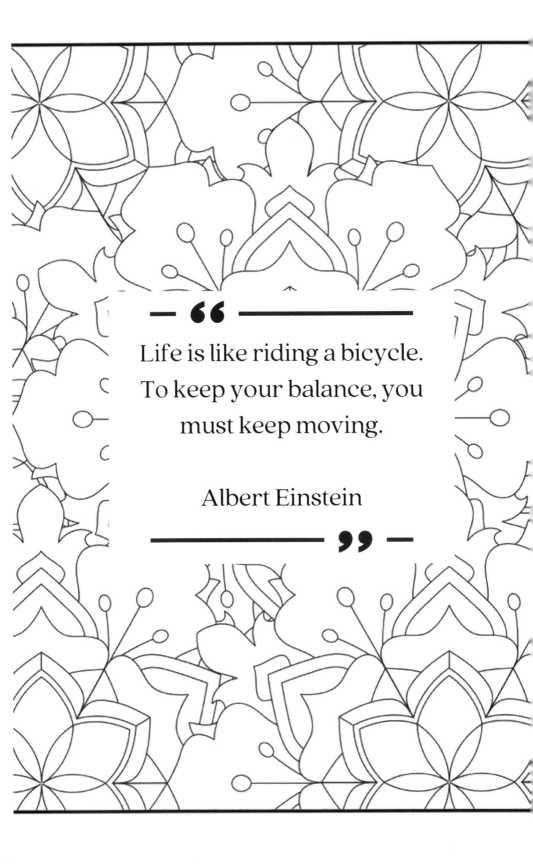

IF YOU HAD NO FEAR TODAY, WHAT WOULD YOU DO?

FREE YOURSELF

WHY?

LET IT GO

WHY NOT?

FREE YOURSELF

WHAT THINGS MAKE YOU REALLY ANGRY? IS THERE A WAY YOU COULD LIMIT YOUR ANGER ABOUT THESE THINGS?

_____

_____

_____

_____

_____

_____

_____

_____

_____

_____

_____

_____

_____

_____

_____

_____

_____

_____

_____

_____

LET IT GO

WHAT THINGS MAKE YOU REALLY HAPPY? HOW CAN YOU BRING THEM INTO YOUR LIFE MORE OFTEN?

_____
_____
_____
_____
_____
_____
_____
_____
_____
_____
_____
_____
_____
_____
_____
_____
_____
_____
_____
_____
_____
_____

FREE YOURSELF

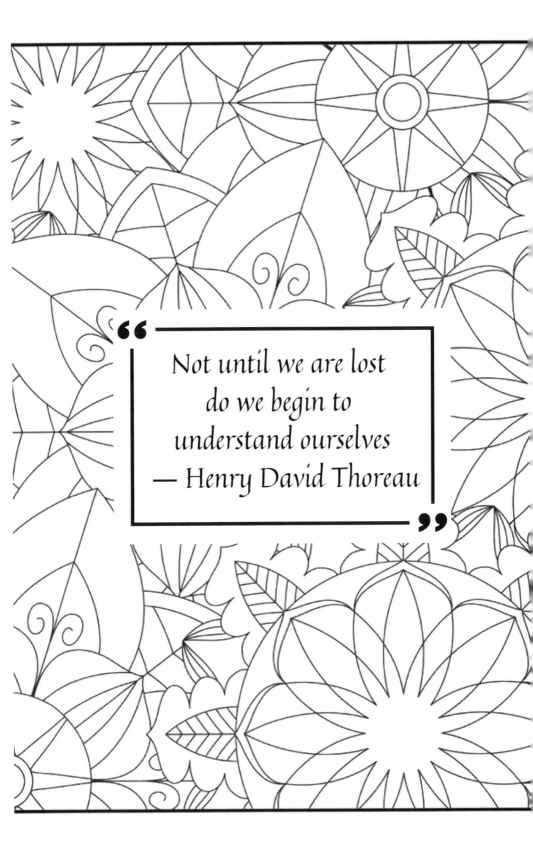

Your brain holds a lot of information. It is not actually meant to hold all of the thoughts, feelings, and stuff you have (or want) to do. Keeping everything in there will only serve to muddle you up. Plus, things are likely to get lost!

A brain dump is really useful for getting everything out of your head onto paper. This section gives you loads of room to do this.

Choose one issue/topic per double page spread. Use the first page (with the shapes) to get everything out in any order that makes sense to you. Once you're finished, write it out in a more logical way, highlighting anything you need to take action on.

Write it out

Write it out

Write it out

Sometimes things happen and we just need a place to vent our anger and frustration. The final section of this journal is designed with exactly that in mind.

The purpose of the Vent Space section is for you to get everything out of your head into a place where there is absolutely no judgement.

You'll find ideas for what you can fill the spaces with at the top of each page. But it's up to you. Use the ideas or ignore them — it is your choice.

This is your Vent Space!

LET GO & JUST SCRIBBLE

FILL THIS PAGE WITH COLORS

FILL THIS PAGE WITH WORDS

FILL THIS PAGE WITH HOW YOU FEEL IN THIS MOMENT

....

DRAW HOW YOU FEEL

WRITE ABOUT HOW YOU FEEL

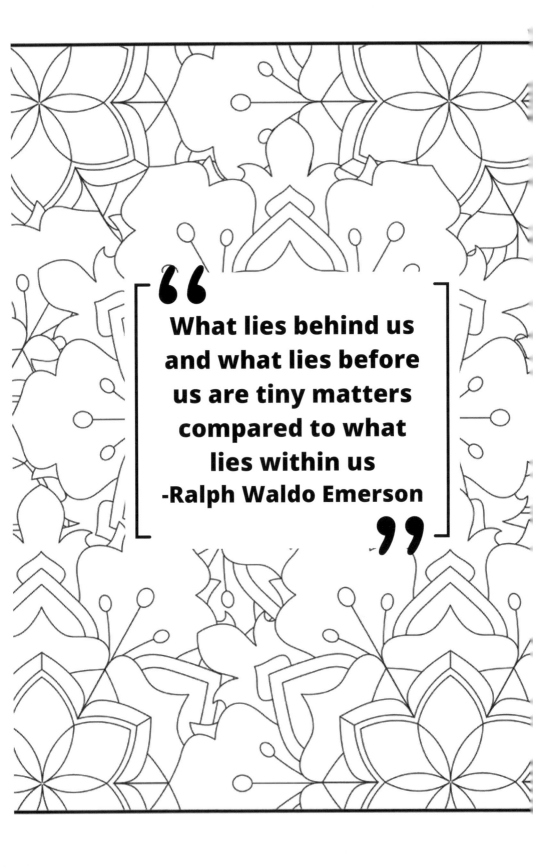

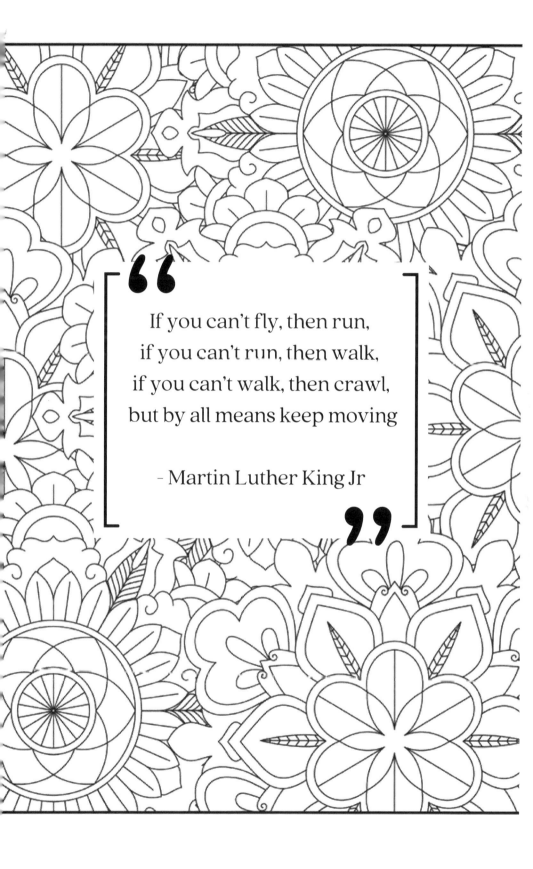

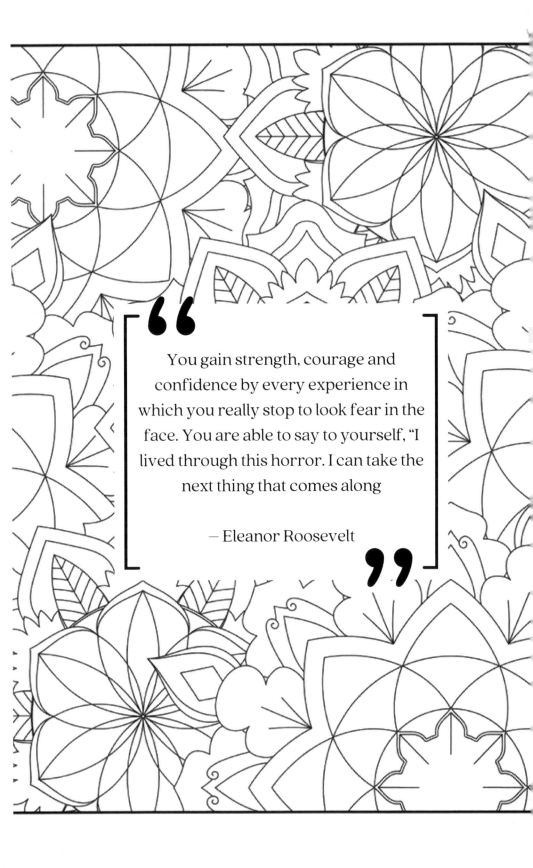

> You gain strength, courage and confidence by every experience in which you really stop to look fear in the face. You are able to say to yourself, "I lived through this horror. I can take the next thing that comes along
>
> – Eleanor Roosevelt

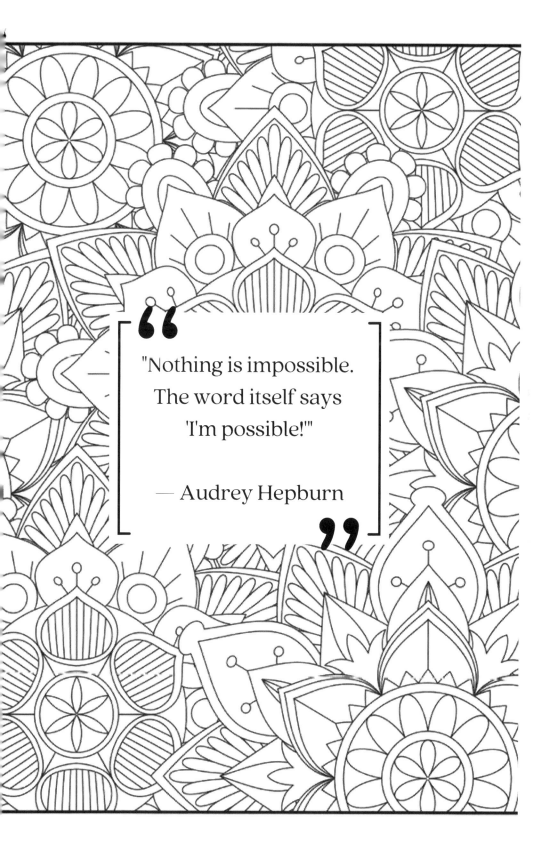

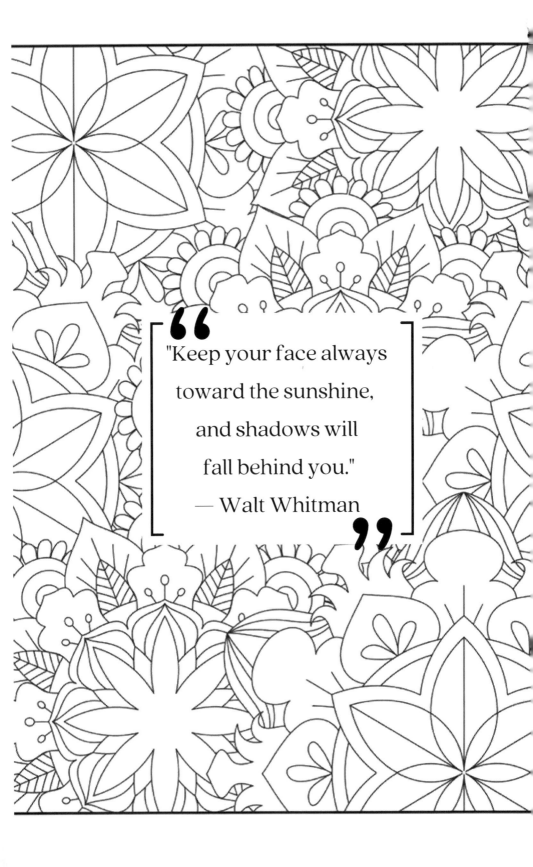

Made in the USA
Columbia, SC
07 November 2023